Contents

Lemon Honey Chicken and Stuffing

MAKES: 6 servings   **PREP:** 15 minutes   **BAKE:** 1 hour

1¾   cups SWANSON® Chicken Stock

2   medium carrots, shredded (about 1 cup)

4   cups PEPPERIDGE FARM® Herb Seasoned Stuffing

6   bone-in chicken breast halves, skin removed

2   tablespoons honey

2   tablespoons lemon juice

1   tablespoon chopped fresh parsley *or* 1 teaspoon dried parsley flakes

3   lemon slices, cut in half

1. Heat the stock and carrots in a 3-quart saucepan over medium heat to a boil. Remove the saucepan from the heat. Add the stuffing and mix lightly.

2. Spoon the stuffing mixture into a greased 3-quart shallow baking dish. Top with the chicken.

3. Bake at 375°F. for 50 minutes.

4. Stir the honey, lemon juice and parsley in a small bowl. Brush the chicken with the honey mixture. Place the lemon slices onto the chicken. Bake for 10 minutes or until the chicken is cooked through.

Broccoli Cheese Chicken & Stuffing

4½ cups PEPPERIDGE FARM® Herb Seasoned Stuffing

2 tablespoons butter, melted

¾ cup water

1 package (10 ounces) frozen chopped broccoli, thawed

6 skinless, boneless chicken breast halves (about 1½ pounds)
  Paprika

1 can (10¾ ounces) CAMPBELL'S® Condensed Broccoli Cheese Soup
  (Regular *or* 98% Fat Free)

⅓ cup milk

1. Crush ½ **cup** stuffing and mix with **1 tablespoon** butter in small bowl. Set aside.

2. Mix water, remaining butter and broccoli in large bowl. Add remaining stuffing and mix lightly. Spoon into 3-quart shallow baking dish. Arrange chicken over stuffing. Sprinkle with paprika.

3. Stir soup and milk in small bowl. Pour over chicken. Sprinkle crushed stuffing mixture over soup mixture.

4. Bake at 400°F. for 40 minutes or until chicken is cooked through.

Quick Pesto Chicken Stuffing Bake

MAKES: 4 servings   **PREP:** 15 minutes   **BAKE:** 25 minutes

1⅓ cups boiling water

  3 tablespoons butter

  1 package (6 ounces) PEPPERIDGE FARM® One Step Chicken Stuffing Mix

  4 skinless, boneless chicken breast halves (about 1 pound)

  2 tablespoons grated Parmesan cheese

  1 tablespoon olive oil *or* vegetable oil

 ¼ teaspoon dried basil leaves, crushed

1. Stir the water, butter and vegetable/seasoning mix from the stuffing package in a large bowl until the butter is melted. Add the stuffing and mix lightly. Let stand for 5 minutes.

2. Spoon the stuffing mixture into a greased 9-inch pie plate. Arrange the chicken over the stuffing mixture.

3. Stir the cheese, oil and basil in a small bowl and spread the mixture evenly over the chicken.

4. Bake at 400°F. for 25 minutes or until chicken is cooked through. Remove the chicken and stir the stuffing.

Easy Chicken Noodle Casserole

MAKES: 4 servings   **PREP:** 10 minutes   **BAKE:** 25 minutes

1 can (10¾ ounces) CAMPBELL'S® Condensed Cream of Chicken Soup (Regular *or* 98% Fat Free)

½ cup milk

1 cup frozen peas

2 cans (4.5 ounces *each*) SWANSON® Premium White Chunk Chicken Breast in Water, drained

2 cups medium egg noodles, cooked and drained

2 tablespoons dry bread crumbs

1 tablespoon butter, melted

1. Stir the soup, milk, peas, chicken and noodles in a 1½-quart casserole. Stir the bread crumbs and butter in a small bowl.

2. Bake at 400°F. for 20 minutes or until the chicken mixture is hot and bubbling. Stir the chicken mixture. Sprinkle with the bread crumb mixture.

3. Bake for 5 minutes or until the topping is golden brown.

Pasta, Cheese & Vegetable Casserole

MAKES: 5 servings   **PREP:** 20 minutes   **BAKE:** 50 minutes

1   can (10¾ ounces) CAMPBELL'S® Condensed Cream of Chicken Soup
    (Regular *or* 98% Fat Free) *or* CAMPBELL'S® Condensed Cream of
    Celery Soup

1½ cups milk

½   teaspoon ground black pepper

1½ cups shredded reduced-fat Cheddar cheese (about 6 ounces)

1½ cups frozen mixed vegetables

4   cups corkscrew-shaped pasta (rotini), cooked and drained

⅓   cup crushed corn flakes

1. Stir the soup, milk, black pepper, cheese, vegetables and pasta in a
2½-quart casserole.

2. Bake at 400°F. for 30 minutes or until the pasta mixture is hot and
bubbling. Stir the pasta mixture. Sprinkle with the corn flakes.

3. Bake for 20 minutes or until the cornflakes are golden brown.

Neapolitan Pasta Shells

MAKES: 4 servings   **PREP:** 20 minutes   **BAKE:** 30 minutes

- 2 tablespoons vegetable oil
- 2 medium zucchini, sliced (about 3 cups)
- 2 cups sliced mushrooms
- 1 medium onion, chopped (about ½ cup)
- ¼ teaspoon ground black pepper
- 2 cups PREGO® Three Cheese Italian Sauce
- ½ of a 16-ounce package medium shell-shaped pasta, cooked and drained (4 cups)
- 1 cup shredded mozzarella cheese

1. Heat the oil in a 3-quart saucepan over medium heat. Add the zucchini, mushrooms, onion and pepper and cook until the vegetables are tender-crisp.

2. Stir the Italian sauce and pasta in the saucepan. Spoon into a 2-quart baking dish. Sprinkle with the cheese.

3. Bake at 350°F. for 30 minutes or until hot and bubbling.

Mac & Cheese Veggie Bake

MAKES: 6 servings   **PREP:** 20 minutes   **BAKE:** 30 minutes

2   cans (10¾ ounces *each*) CAMPBELL'S® Condensed Cheddar Cheese Soup

1½ cups milk

2   tablespoons Dijon-style mustard

1½ cups frozen sugar snap peas

1   medium green *or* red pepper, diced (about 1 cup)

3   cups elbow macaroni, cooked and drained

¼   cup water

2   tablespoons butter, melted

4   cups PEPPERIDGE FARM® Corn Bread Stuffing

1. Stir the soup, milk, mustard, snap peas, pepper and macaroni in a 3-quart shallow baking dish.

2. Stir the water and butter in a large bowl. Add the stuffing and mix lightly to coat. Sprinkle the stuffing over the macaroni mixture.

3. Bake at 400°F. for 30 minutes or until it's hot and bubbling.

Glazed Pork Chops with Corn Stuffing

MAKES: 6 servings   **PREP:** 15 minutes   **BAKE:** 30 minutes

1¾ cups SWANSON® Chicken Stock

⅛ teaspoon ground red pepper

1 cup frozen whole kernel corn

1 stalk celery, chopped (about ½ cup)

1 medium onion, chopped (about ½ cup)

4 cups PEPPERIDGE FARM® Corn Bread Stuffing

   Vegetable cooking spray

6 boneless pork chops, ¾-inch thick (about 1½ pounds)

2 tablespoons packed brown sugar

2 teaspoons spicy-brown mustard

1. Heat the stock, red pepper, corn, celery and onion in a 3-quart saucepan over medium heat to a boil. Remove the saucepan from the heat. Add the stuffing and mix lightly.

2. Spray a 3-quart shallow baking dish with the cooking spray. Spoon the stuffing into the baking dish. Top with the pork. Stir the brown sugar and mustard in a small bowl until the mixture is smooth. Spread the brown sugar mixture over the pork.

3. Bake at 400°F. for 30 minutes or until the pork is cooked through.

Classic Lasagna

MAKES: 12 servings   **PREP:** 30 minutes   **BAKE:** 30 minutes   **STAND:** 10 minutes

 3 cups ricotta cheese

12 ounces shredded mozzarella cheese (about 3 cups)

 ¾ cup grated Parmesan cheese

 2 eggs

 1 pound ground beef

 1 jar (45 ounces) PREGO® Three Cheese Italian Sauce

12 lasagna noodles, cooked and drained

1. Stir the ricotta cheese, mozzarella cheese, ½ **cup** Parmesan cheese and eggs in a medium bowl and set it aside.

2. In a 3-quart saucepan over medium-high heat, cook the beef until it's well browned, stirring often to separate the meat. Pour off any fat. Stir the Italian sauce in the saucepan.

3. Spoon **1 cup** meat mixture in each of two 2-quart shallow baking dishes. Top **each** with **2** lasagna noodles and **about 1¼ cups** cheese mixture. Repeat the layers. Top with the remaining **2** lasagna noodles, remaining meat mixture and the Parmesan cheese.

4. Bake at 400°F. for 30 minutes or it's until hot and bubbling. Let stand for 10 minutes.

tip

To freeze, prepare lasagna but do not bake. Cover tightly with foil and freeze. Bake frozen lasagna, uncovered, at 350°F. for 1 hour 15 minutes or until hot. Or, refrigerate 24 hours to thaw. Bake thawed lasagna, uncovered, at 350°F. for 50 minutes or until hot. Let stand for 10 minutes.

Beef and Cornbread Bake

MAKES: 6 servings   **PREP:** 15 minutes   **BAKE:** 25 minutes   **STAND:** 10 minutes

1 pound ground beef

1 teaspoon dried oregano leaves, crushed

¾ cup PACE® Picante Sauce

1 can (about 8 ounces) tomato sauce

1 can (about 16 ounces) whole kernel corn, drained

½ cup shredded Cheddar cheese (2 ounces)

1 package (about 8 ounces) corn muffin mix

1. Cook the beef and oregano in a 10-inch skillet over medium-high heat until the beef is well browned, stirring often to separate the meat. Pour off any fat.

2. Stir the picante sauce, tomato sauce and corn in the skillet. Cook until the mixture is hot and bubbling. Stir in the cheese. Pour the beef mixture into a 2-quart shallow baking dish.

3. Mix the corn muffin mix according to the package directions. Spread the batter over the beef mixture.

4. Bake at 375°F. for 25 minutes or until the crust is golden brown. Let stand for 10 minutes before serving.

Beef 'n' Bean Bake

MAKES: 4 servings   **PREP:** 10 minutes   **BAKE:** 30 minutes

  1 **pound ground beef**

  1 **can (19 ounces) CAMPBELL'S® CHUNKY™ Roadhouse-Beef & Bean Chili**

  ¾ **cup PACE® Picante Sauce**

  ¾ **cup water**

  8 **corn tortillas (6-inch), cut into 1-inch pieces**

  ⅔ **cup shredded Cheddar cheese**

1. Heat the oven to 400°F.

2. Cook the beef in a 10-inch skillet over medium-high heat until well browned, stirring often to separate the meat. Pour off any fat.

3. Stir the chili, picante sauce, water, tortillas and **half** the cheese in the skillet. Pour the beef mixture into a 2-quart shallow baking dish. Cover the baking dish.

4. Bake for 30 minutes or until the mixture is hot and bubbling. Sprinkle with the remaining cheese.

Fall Confetti Oven Baked Risotto

MAKES: 6 servings   **PREP:** 5 minutes   **BAKE:** 50 minutes

1 can (10¾ ounces) CAMPBELL'S® Condensed Cream of Chicken with Herbs Soup

3¼ cups water

1¼ cups *uncooked* regular long-grain white rice

1 small carrot, shredded (about ⅓ cup)

¼ cup frozen peas

⅓ cup grated Parmesan cheese

1. Stir the soup, water, rice, carrot and peas in a 2-quart casserole. **Cover**.

2. Bake at 375°F. for 50 minutes or until rice is tender. Stir in the cheese. (Risotto will absorb liquid as it stands.)

Greek Rice Bake

MAKES: 6 servings   **PREP:** 15 minutes   **BAKE:** 40 minutes   **STAND:** 5 minutes

- 1 can (10¾ ounces) CAMPBELL'S® Condensed Cream of Mushroom Soup (Regular *or* 98% Fat Free)
- ½ cup water
- 1 can (about 14.5 ounces) diced tomatoes, undrained
- 1 jar (6 ounces) marinated artichoke hearts, drained and cut in half
- 2 portobello mushrooms, coarsely chopped (about 2 cups)
- ¾ cup *uncooked* quick-cooking brown rice
- 1 can (about 15 ounces) small white beans, rinsed and drained
- 3 to 4 tablespoons crumbled feta cheese

1. Heat the oven to 400°F. Stir the soup, water, tomatoes, artichokes, mushrooms, rice and beans in a 2-quart casserole. Cover the casserole.

2. Bake for 40 minutes or until the rice is tender. Stir the rice mixture. Let stand for 5 minutes. Sprinkle with the cheese before serving.

tip

Different brands of quick-cooking brown rice cook differently, so the bake time for this recipe may be slightly longer or shorter than indicated.

Ham and Asparagus Strata

MAKES: 8 servings   **PREP:** 15 minutes   **BAKE:** 45 minutes   **STAND:** 5 minutes

- 4 cups PEPPERIDGE FARM® Cubed Country Style Stuffing
- 2 cups shredded Swiss cheese (about 8 ounces)
- 1½ cups cooked cut asparagus
- 1½ cups cubed cooked ham
- 1 can (10¾ ounces) CAMPBELL'S® Condensed Cream of Asparagus Soup *or* CAMPBELL'S® Condensed Cream of Mushroom Soup
- 2 cups milk
- 5 eggs
- 1 tablespoon Dijon-style mustard

1. Heat the oven to 350°F. Stir the stuffing, cheese, asparagus and ham in a greased 3-quart shallow baking dish.

2. Beat the soup, milk, eggs and mustard in a medium bowl with a fork or whisk. Pour over the stuffing mixture. Stir and press the stuffing mixture into the milk mixture to coat.

3. Bake for 45 minutes or until a knife inserted in the center comes out clean. Let stand for 5 minutes.

tip

*For 1½ **cups** cooked cut asparagus, use ¾ **pound** fresh asparagus, trimmed and cut into 1-inch pieces **or 1 package** (about 10 ounces) frozen asparagus spears, thawed, drained and cut into 1-inch pieces.*